LIFE OF ST. ONUPHRIUS

St. Salonius of Geneva

Translated by: D.P. Curtin

Copyright @ 2007 Dalcassian Publishing Company

All rights reserved. No part of this publication may be reproduced, distributed, or transmitted in any form or by any means, including photocopying, recording, or other electronic or mechanical methods, without the prior written permission of the publisher, except in the case of brief quotations embodied in critical reviews and certain other non-commercial uses permitted by copyright law. For permission request, write to Dalcassian Publishing Company at dalcassianpublishing at gmail.com

ISBN: 979-8-8692-4075-0 (Paperback)

Library of Congress Control Number:
Author: Curtin, D.P. (1985-)

Printed by Ingram Content Group, 1 Ingram Blvd, La Vergne, Tennessee

First printing edition 2007.

LIFE OF ST. ONUPHRIUS

Prologue by an anonymous translator.

I recently found the Life of Blessed Onuphrius written among the commentaries of the Greeks, as I once learned from a venerable and wise man, that is, Gregory, narrating his deeds. Paphnutius, also a most holy man, revealed this in the Greek language from the beginning. Whom I followed, I translated from Greek into Latin, giving to the Lord, that his probable life, manifested according to my powers, should give astonishment and admiration to the readers. Do not judge, I beseech you, the rusticity of my speech, but turn to patience with such a spirit of labor: which a man full of God endured patiently, while he despised the glory of worldly vanity, and inherited the heavenly kingdom by living in poverty.

LIFE

Of blessed memory, Paphnutius thus revealed some of the secrets of his thoughts and actions, saying:

CHAPTER 1.--One day, while I, Paphnutius, was sitting alone and silent, I thought in my heart that I should seek the deserts, and survey all the places of the holy monks, their pious behavior, and consider how they ministered to God. Wherefore it came to pass that I took my way in silence and hastened into the wilderness at a desirable speed. I therefore took bread and a little water with me, so that I might not faint from the labor of the journey. But at the end of the fourth day, the victuals which I had taken with me failed, and my limbs, being refreshed by no food, lost their strength. And soon, by divine grace, the impending death was taken away; and having recovered my strength, I set out on my journey, and spent the next four days without tasting anything. When these things were finished, I lay prostrate on the ground, as though dead. Immediately also, comforted by a heavenly helper, I saw a man assisting me, whose glory was wonderful, whose splendor was terrible, whose beauty was praiseworthy, whose stature was noble, and whose appearance was excellent. As I looked at him, I was greatly astonished; but still he approached with a calm countenance, now touched my hands, now my lips, and powerfully restored my strength (John 3:12). Immediately I got up joyfully, and with the favor of God, I directed a course of seventeen days through the desert, until I arrived at the place which the Lord had provided to show me to his unworthy servant; I stopped there from the labor of the journey.

CHAPTER 2.--Therefore, while I was resting tired and thinking how hard I had gone, I saw a man in the distance, terrifying in appearance, surrounded on all sides like the hair of a beast; whose hair was so profuse, that his body was covered with their diffusion. For clothing he also used leaves and herbs, with which he only girdled the lower part of the kidney. When I saw such a man, I was greatly frightened with terror, troubled beyond belief with fear and wonder, since such a wonderful form had never before my eyes been shown in human form. I did not know what to do; but as much as I could, I sought flight, and ascended a nearby mountain at a rapid pace; and there I fell trembling and hid myself from his face under a thicket of leaves, giving many sighs. 100 I almost failed with age and with the labor of abstinence. Now when he saw me lying on the mountain, he cried out with a loud voice, and said: Man of God, come down from the mountain. Do not be afraid; for I am a susceptible man, like you. Having therefore been comforted by these words, I recovered my mind, and soon I went down and came to the holy man and prostrated myself at his feet in fear. He, too, forbidding me to lie down before him, says, Arise, arise; for you are the servant of God, and you are called Paphnutius, the friend of the saints. I arose immediately; and although weary, yet I sat before him joyfully, already with fervent desire, who he was, and what his life was, desiring to know, saying: Behold, he has fulfilled his vow, who led me through this wilderness. But my dying frame feels some comfort, but my thirsty mind has not yet found refreshment. For this reason, I beseech you, elder, with a devoted heart, and through him, for whose love you live in the deserts of this solitude, I challenge you, that whence you are, or what your name is, or when you arrive here, you will tell me in open words. And the man of God recognizing how willingly I was to hear the opinion of his work, said to me:

CHAPTER 3.--Since I see you, dear brother, with an eager mind to know the long travails of my life, do not hesitate to repeat these to you from the beginning. I, though undeserved, call Onuphrius. And behold, it is not less than seventy years that I have labored in this desert. I conversed more often with the beasts, I ate the fruits of herbs for bread, I laid my miserable body in the mountains and in the caves and in the valleys. For so many years I looked at no one but you alone, I took food from no man, I was nourished in the monastery called Hermopolis, in the province named Thebaid, where at the same time lived nearly a hundred monks. Moreover, their life was such that they all lived equanimously in manners and actions, and with one heart and one spirit, submitted their necks to the yoke and discipline of the holy rule, and did not at all fear the waves of this world. Whatever was pleasing to one, was pleasing to all. With a holy mind, pure faith, and perfect charity, they walked before God, whom they did not cease to serve day and night with all meekness and patience. Such was their silence and self-restraint, that no one dared to utter a word except with a just question, or a right answer. There, too, I received the fodder of holy doctrine from my youth; there I learned the rule of a regular life from my brothers, by whom I was dearly loved; I was carefully instructed by them how I should keep the institutions of God's commandments.

CHAPTER 4.--Indeed, I have heard my venerable brothers frequently praise the life of our blessed Father Elijah, who endeavored to afflict himself in the desert in such abstinence and prayer that he deserved to receive the greatest strength from the Lord; and being transported in a chariot of fire, the holy spirit imparted to the disciple the gifts which he had, and still being a very old man, he did not see the penalty of death. Moreover, as an example, they brought forward the blessed John the Baptist, who shone out most famously in the series of the New Testament, and for many years, having been entrusted with divine office, soaked his body, until he was worthy to baptize the Redeemer of the world in the waves of the Jordan, and he showed with his finger that he was the Lamb of God.

CHAPTER V.--But when I heard them reciting such things, I said to them: Why, my elders, do you marvel at their life and miracles? or why are their deeds so constantly mentioned? Are those who dwell in the desert stronger than you, or lighter? But they answered and said: Sons, they are stronger than us, because they live without human helpers. Therefore, we are seen one by the other, and the divine office is celebrated by us at the same time. If we ever want food, we find it ready; if at any time infirmity or any infirmity of the body creeps in, the care of the brethren immediately helps us with all concern. We live in light-built buildings, in which we are sheltered from the heat of the sun, and from the flood of rain, and from the whirlwind of wind and storm. As for the monks who are in the desert, they receive no consolation except from God. If at any time they have suffered hardships or tribulations, or have begun to fight with the devil, the ancient enemy of the human race, who stands by them? by whom are they assisted? But to those who lack human comfort, it is clear that they have a divine one. And if they are hungry, who will give them bread? If they are thirsty, who will give them water, where there is no bread and water? There is no doubt that the greatest labor is in desert places, where nothing is found necessary. First, then, when they decide to live in solitude, they strive to stand firmly in the fear of God. In hunger and thirst, in labor and suffering, they torture their bodies; they fight manfully against diabolical plots; and in order to win, they fight with spiritual swords against the fiery weapons of the wicked. Indeed, that ancient enemy, the inventor of all iniquity, endeavors to subvert them, and to involve them in the company of his malice, and to withdraw them from the good will which they had begun; and entangle their minds again with worldly pleasures, so that they may persevere in the work begun. Almighty God, therefore, who does not abandon those who hope in him, surrounds them with the weapons of his power, so that the invasion of Satan will not be able to prostrate them, who are protected by the highness of divine mercy. For this reason, the angels of God are constantly sent to them, and by their hands whatever things are necessary are more frequently administered to them. They draw water from the rock, which is interpreted as Christ. For it is written: The saints who hope in the Lord will have strength, they will take wings like eagles; they shall fly, and shall not fail; they will run, and their steps will not slip (Is. 40). And elsewhere: Those who are thirsty are nourished from the fountain above, and the leaves of herbs are sweet in their mouths like a honeycomb. But if at any time the devil wrestles against them, they immediately rise up: they spread their hands to the Lord, they faithfully pour out their prayers before the divine majesty; soon they are lifted up by heavenly help, and the treacherous arrows of the enemy are completely destroyed. Do you not understand, my son, how it is read in Psalm: For the poor will not be forgotten to the end, the patience of the poor will not perish forever (Ps. 9)? And again: The Lord heard them on the day of trouble and delivered them from all distress (Ps. 16). For each one will receive his own reward, according to his labor (1 Cor. 3). For blessed is the man who is always fearful and does the will of God in this present life and is diligent in his frailty (Pro. 28). Know most assuredly, O son, that the angels of God minister to holy and righteous men every day, and that their bodies and souls are continually illuminated by heavenly power.

CHAPTER 6.--Finally, with such reasoning, I, poor Onuphrius, carefully instructed by the most holy Fathers in my monastery, began to consider with a silent mind what glorious happiness is enjoyed in the heavens by those who endured laborious struggles on earth for the love of the Lord: my heart was burning, my mind was burning with longing for the joys of the world to break away, to draw near with all one's strength to the heavenly country, as the Psalmist teaches, saying: But it is good for me to cling to God, to put my hope in the Lord God (Ps. 72).

CHAPTER 7.--And while I was thinking these things anxiously, I got up in a hurry in the silence of the night, I brought with me a little bread with a little vegetables, so that it would hardly suffice until the fourth day; and so according to the dispensation of God and his piety I went, that he might show me the place of my dwelling. But when I left the monastery in the mountains, I went into the desert; and thinking that I should remain there, immediately I saw a bright light before me, as if meeting me. When I saw this, I was very afraid. For this reason also I thought that I must return to the monastery from whence I came. And immediately from a ray of brilliant light a most beautiful man came to me and said to me: Do not be afraid, for I am an angel of God, destined by divine providence to guard you from your birth, so that I may remain with you at the command of God, and lead you into this desert. Be perfect, walk humbly before the Lord, labor with joy, keep your heart in every guard, live without complaint, persevere in good work. But I will not leave thee until I offer thy soul in the presence of the highest majesty. These things the angel spoke to me, who accompanied me on the journey.

CHAPTER 8.--We continued in this way together for six or seven miles, and we came to a certain very beautiful cave. I approached, wanting to break open in case anyone remained inside. According to the custom of the monks, I began to cry, and humbly asked for a blessing. From there I saw a most holy man come out, whom I worshiped prostrate on the ground. But he stretched out his hands to me, raised me from the ground, gave me a kiss of peace, and said: "For thou art my brother, the co-operator of the hermit's life, O son, enter in." May God grant you that the fear of him may continue in you, that your work may be pleasing in his sight. I immediately entered the cave with him, and stayed several days with him, desiring to learn his works, and to investigate more curiously his solitary dwelling; he too, recognizing my desire, offered me an honorable counsel; and how I should overcome the devil's scheming, he graciously explained in charitable words. After some days had passed, he admonished me with such words, saying: My son, arise, go with me; you must enter the interior of the desert, and dwell alone in another cave: there, if you fight manfully, you will overcome all the temptations of the demons. Therefore, God wants to test you in this desert, if you are willing to faithfully obey his commandments. All his commandments are faithful, confirmed for ever and ever, made in truth and equity (Ps. 100). And when the holy man had said these things, he arose, and went with me into the interior of the desert for four days' journey. But on the fifth day we came to a place called Calidiomea, where there were palm trees nearby. Then the man of God said: Behold, my son, see the place which the Lord has prepared for you to dwell in. And he was with me for the space of thirty days, teaching me to keep the doctrine of God's commandments with careful care. After these things had been done, he commended me to the Lord with his holy prayer. and separated from me, he returned to his own. But every year he was wont to visit me, and never ceased to remind me with divine addresses of what energy and simplicity I ought to live.

CHAPTER 9.--But at a certain time, coming to me according to custom, between words of greeting he fell prostrate on the ground. When I saw that, I was very sad; and falling on the ground, I wept profusely with tears. I immediately received his body, and otherwise commended Calidiome to the earth.

CHAPTER 10.--And while I, Paphnutius, was listening to the discourse of this reason from the most holy man Onuphrius, I said to him: Holy father, I already feel that the labor which you have endured for the name of Christ in this desert is not small. The holy man answered: Believe me, my dearest brother: I endured in the desert, so that I often thought that I would be overcome by death. You look forward to many times in life, so that I could hardly feel the breath in my body. During the day I was scorched by the heat and fire of the burning sun, during the night I was wet with dew and frost and lacked hunger and thirst. Oh, how much and how much I have suffered! It is not enough, nor is it proper for anyone to recount the plagues and labors which a man who is about to die must endure for the love of the living God. The Lord will reward the labors of his saints (Wis. 10). Whose riches, as they are not increased, so will in no way be diminished. For through him I endured hunger, thirst, cold and heat, and the torments of many kinds of troubles, he is able to comfort me with heavenly riches among the company of angels: but I despised corporeal food, that I might receive spiritual things worthily. For the holy angel daily offered me bread, and served me water as a measure, that my body might be strengthened, that it might not fail, and that it might persevere continually in the praise of God. Palm trees were established there, which sprouted fruit twelve times a year. Collecting these every day, I ate them for bread, mixed with the leaves of herbs, and they were in my mouth like a honeycomb. For in the Gospel, we read: Man does not live by bread alone, but by every word that proceeds from the mouth of God (Matt. 4). Brother Paphnutus, if you seek to fulfill the will of God, everything you need is prepared by him. Wherefore Truth itself admonishes, saying: Be not anxious for your soul what you shall eat, or what you shall drink, nor for your body what you shall put on, for your Father knows that you need all these things. Seek ye first the kingdom of God, and his righteousness, and all these things shall be added unto you (Matt. 6).

CHAPTER 11.--And when I had listened more intently to this from the blessed man Onuphrius, marveling at his words and actions and labors, I said: Father kindly, on Sunday or Saturday did you receive communion from anyone? But he answered and said: Every Sunday or Saturday I find an angel of the Lord ready, bearing with him the most holy body and blood of our Lord Jesus Christ: from whose hand I receive the most precious gifts, and the perpetual salvation of my life. It is also true that all those who lead a spiritual life in the hermitage of monks share in such joy. But these holy hermits, who dwell in this solitude, if perhaps they ever desire to see a man, are at once carried up to heaven by an angel: there they see a vision of the souls of the righteous, shining like the sun in the kingdom of their Father, there they behold a multitude of angels, and their souls mingled with the company of the blessed. Wherefore all those who contend in the race, with all their minds, with all their hearts, and with all their strength, fervent in good work, in so far as they deserve to possess the glory of the heavenly country with Christ and with the saints. In short, I learned all these things, as the venerable Onuphrius related them, near the top of the very hill, where he met me. My joy was so filled that I forgot all the adversity I had encountered on the way.

CHAPTER 12.--I believe, I say, Father, that I am deputed among the happy, because I have earned to see you and your excellent works. Your words are very beautiful, sweetened with all sweetness, so they penetrate the innermost parts of my heart, so that I can say with the Psalmist: How sweet your words are to my mouth, above honey and honeycomb to my mouth (Ps. 118). He said: Son, go with me; Look at the place of my dwelling, let us spare a few words. He immediately got up, went ahead, and I followed. He took me with him on a journey of about three miles: we came to Calidiomea, a spiritual place, gracefully adorned with palm trees. There we poured out our prayers to the Lord; and having completed them, we sat down on the ground, disputing in divine discourses. And when the sun had set, I saw bread laid out with a little water. Indeed, the man of God, sensing that I was getting tired, said to me: Indeed, my son, I see that you are in danger unless you take food. So, get up and eat. To whom I say: The Lord lives (3 Kings 17), and blessed be the Lord my God, in whose presence we shall be; I will neither eat nor drink, until we both take food with pure charity. So, I hardly drove him to do what I wanted. Nevertheless, as he recognized my desire, he broke the bread and gave it to me; we ate, and we were full, and there were leftovers for us to eat. We spent that night almost sleepless, and we were drenched in divine praises.

CHAPTER 13.--In the morning, after an hour of prayer, I saw his face so changed from pallor, and I asked him what had happened. He said: Do not be dismayed, brother Paphnutus, since Almighty God has directed you to take the right path into this wilderness, that you may bury me honorably, and commit my body to the earth. Indeed, at this hour the soul is freed from the bonds of the flesh and is transported to its creator in the heavenly kingdom. Most loving brother, (for I know your desire) when you return to Egypt, remember me in the presence of your brothers, and in the presence of all who worship Christ. This is my demand, which I obtained from the Lord God. If anyone sacrifices an offering for the love of my name before the sight of our Lord Jesus Christ, and to his praise, he will be freed from every temptation of the devil and from the bond of human depravity and will become capable of an eternal inheritance with the holy angels in the kingdom of heaven. But if anyone is not able to offer an offering, or to redeem because of want, let him give alms to the poor in the name of the Lord and in honor of him, and I will pray for him in the sight of God, that he may be worthy to enjoy the heavenly life above. If anyone is unable to offer either offering or alms, for my charity let him burn incense to the Lord our God for a sweet smell, and I pray for him that he may possess everlasting joy. To whom I say: My father, do not be angry if I speak: If no one has incense, nor any ability, whence he can appease God, so that he does not lack your blessing, in whatever trouble he calls on you? Then he answered: If any poor man in the desert, or in any other place, has not an offering or alms, or incense to sacrifice, let him rise up, and stretch out his hands to the Lord, and say the Sunday prayer three times, that is, Our Father, for me with a concentrated mind , and sings in the name of the Holy Trinity. But I intercede for him with the Lord, that he may deserve to become a partaker of the heavenly life with all the saints of God.

CHAPTER 14.--Again I said to him: Lord, if I were worthy, or if it were permitted to me by the gifts of your grace, after your death I would very willingly occupy this place. But he said: Nothing is permitted to you, my son, and it was not for this reason that God sent you to wander in this solitude, that you might obtain a dwelling-place here; but that you may be congratulated with the righteous who are in the wilderness; and endeavor to make known to the world those things which you learned in the desert. Go to Egypt: stay there until the end of your life; do a good work, and you will receive a crown of everlasting glory.

CHAPTER 15.--When this man of God was speaking, I rolled at his feet, saying: Dear father, for I know that whatever you ask of God, the Lord will give you because of the immense labor of the long struggle, with which you afflicted your body for seventy years in the name of the Lord; grant me, therefore, the gifts of your holy blessing, in so far as I may become like you in virtue, and by your intervention my spirit may be directed, and I may deserve to share with you in the future. He who immediately answered on the contrary, said these things: Paphnutus, do not be sad: your request, giving thanks to the Lord, will be stable. Stand in the faith, act manfully, raise your eyes with your mind to God, strengthen yourself in the commandments, strive vigorously to do good, and lay hold on eternal life (1 Cor. 16). May the angels of God protect you and preserve you from every plan of wickedness, so that you may be found pure before God and spotless on the day of his examination. After these things he got up and prayed to the Lord with tears, bent his knees, and suddenly said: Into your hands, God, I commend my spirit. And when he had said these things, a splendid light overshadowed his body, and in the brightness of the light his holy soul was dissolved in flesh.

CHAPTER 16.--Suddenly I heard the voice of many angels praising God, and in the departure of the most holy soul of Saint Onuphrius, the ethereal echoes of the angelic song brought inexpressible joy to the stars, through which the

LIFE OF ST. ONUPHRIUS

heavenly hosts brought the soul of the illustrious soldier to heaven. Soon my eyes overflowed with tears, my inward groans produced, streams of tears flowed, my lamentations for poor Paphnutius overflowed: I wept bitterly, because I could no longer hold him whom I had scarcely found. Then I tore my tunic in half, put it on one side, placed the blessed body in the other, and buried it in a tomb that had been cut out of the rock. Then, seeing that I was left alone, I began to mourn again. So, I got up in mourning, and wanted to enter his cave. Finally, while I was standing, the cave itself fell with a great crash, and the palm trees, uprooted, fell together. I, Paphnutius, therefore knew that it was not the Lord's will that I should dwell in that place; I departed thence and returned to Egypt: and there I reported to the church what I had seen and heard.

Saint Onuphrius therefore died in the month of June, on the eleventh day, that is, on the 3rd day of the same month. There his benefits are guaranteed even to the present day: to the praise and glory of our Lord Jesus Christ, to whom is honor and power forever and ever. Amen.

LATIN TEXT

LIFE OF ST. ONUPHRIUS

Prologus interpretis anonymi.

Beati Onuphrii Vitam inter Graecorum commenta scriptam nuper reperi, ut quondam a venerabili ac prudentissimo viro, scilicet Gregorio, ipsius gesta narrante, cognovi. Hanc Paphnutius, vir quoque sanctissimus, Graeco sermone retexit ab exordio. Quem ego secutus, e Graeco transtuli in Latinum, largiente Domino, ut ejus probabilis vita secundum vires meas manifestata, admirationem legentibus praebeat et imilationem. Non perpendite, quaeso, mei sermonis rusticitatem, sed tanti laboris animo revolvite longanimitatem: quam vir Deo plenus patienter sustinuit, dum mundanae vanitatis gloriam sprevit, et coeleste regnum districte vivendo sibimet haereditavit.

VITA.

Beatae memoriae Paphnutius quaedam cogitationum et actuum suorum secreta taliter reservavit, dicens.

CAP. I.--Quodam die, dum ego Paphnutius solus tacitusque sederem, cogitavi in corde meo quod deserta peterem, et universa loca sanctorum monachorum, piaeque conversationis habitum lustrarem, ac qualiter Deo ministrarent, considerarem. Unde factum est ut tacitus iter arriperem, et in eremum cursu desiderabili properarem. Panes itaque cum aqua exigua mecum portavi, ne deficerem a labore itineris coepti. Quarto autem die peracto, alimenta quae mecum sumpsi defecerunt, meaque membra nullo victu refocillata vires perdiderunt. Moxque divina illustrante gratia, mors imminens ablata est; assumptisque viribus iter arripui, atque dies alios quatuor nihil gustando peregi. His itaque completis, nimium fessus, humo prostratus jacui velut mortuus. Extemplo quoque coelesti solatus adjutorio, assistere mihi vidi virum, gloria mirabilem, splendore terribilem, pulchritudine laudabilem, magnitudine procerum, aspectu praeclarum. Quem ut aspexi, vehementer obstupui; sed tamen ille vultu placido accedens, nunc manus, nunc labia mea tetigit, mihique vires potenter restauravit (Joannes, libello III, n. 12). Continuo laetus surrexi, Deoque favente, per solitudinem exinde decem et septem dierum cursum direxi, quousque ad locum quem Dominus mihi famulo suo indigno providebat ostendere, perveni; illic ab itineris labore cessavi.

CAP. II.--Igitur dum fessus requiescerem, et quam aegre profectus essem cogitarem, virum procul aspectu terribilem vidi, in modum bestiae pilis undique circumseptum; cui tanta scilicet capillorum prolixitas erat, ut corpus illius ipsorum diffusione tegeretur. Pro vestimento quoque foliis herbisque utebatur, quibus subteriora renum tantummodo cingebat. Tali viso homine, nimio perterritus sum terrore, anxiatus ultra quam credi potest timore et admiratione, quoniam tam mira forma meis oculis nunquam fuit ostensa in humana specie. Quid facerem ignoravi; sed quantum valui, fugam petii, montemque propinquum concito cursu ascendi; ibique tremefactus corrui, atque me sub frondium densitate a facie illius abscondi, multa dans suspiria. 100 Defeci pene aetate et labore abstinentiae. Hic vero dum me cernebat in monte jacentem, voce nimia clamavit, et dixit: Vir Dei, descende de monte. Noli timere; ego enim sum homo passibilis, tibi similis. His itaque consolatus verbis, mentem recipi, moxque descendi, et ad virum sanctum perveni, atque pedibus ejus me timidus prostravi. Ille quoque me prohibens ante se jacere, Surge, inquit, surge; tu enim es Dei servus, et vocaris Paphnutius, sanctorum amicus. Statim surrexi; et quamvis fessus, tamen laetus ante eum sedi, jam ferventi desiderio, quis ipse, et qualis ejus esset vita, cupiens dignoscere, dicens: Ecce votum adimplevit, qui me per hanc eremum direxit. En artus mei fatiscentes aliquod sentiunt solatium, sed mens sitibunda non adhuc invenit refrigerium. Idcirco te, senior, corde devoto deprecor, atque per illum, ob cujus amorem hujus solitudinis deserta habitas, te contestor, ut unde sis aut quomodo voceris, seu quando huc adveneris, apertis mihi verbis denunties. Et vir Dei recognoscens quam libenti animo sententiam sui laboris audirem, dixit mihi:

CAP. III.--Quoniam te, frater dilecte, avida mente vitae meae longas aerumnas velle scire video, repetere me tibi non dubites has ab exordio. Ego, licet immeritus, vocor Onuphrius. Et ecce non minus sunt quam septuaginta anni, quod in hoc deserto laboriose vixi. Cum feris conversatus sum crebrius, pro pane comedi jugiter herbarum fructus, in montibus et in speluncis et in vallibus meum reclinavi miserabile corpus. Tot annis neminem nisi te solum adspexi, alimentum a nullo hominum sumpsi, in monasterio Hermopolim dicto nutritus, in provincia Thebaida nominata, ubi simul pene centum monachi degebant. Porro vita illorum talis exstitit, ut more et actione aequanimiter omnes viverent, et uno corde et uno spiritu, jugo ac disciplinae sanctae regulae colla submitterent, atque fluctus hujus saeculi omnino non formidarent. Quidquid uni placebat, cunctis placebat. Mente sancta, fide pura, charitate perfecta ante Deum incedebant, cui die noctuque omni mansuetudine et patientia ministrare non cessabant. Tanta his erat taciturnitas cum abstinentia, ut nullus auderet nisi cum justa interrogatione, vel recto responso, reddere verbum. Ibi quoque pabulum sanctae doctrinae ab adolescentia suscepi; ibi regularis vitae normam a fratribus didici, a quibus amabiliter diligebar; ab his, qualiter instituta mandatorum Dei servare deberem, diligenter instruebar.

CAP. IV.--Profecto vitam beati Patris nostri Eliae venerabiles fratres meos audivi frequenter laudare, qui se in eremo in tanta abstinentia et oratione studuit affligere, ut maximam virtutem a Domino meruisset accipere; et igneo curru transvectus, spiritus sancti dona quae habuerat, discipulo impartiri, ac adhuc longaevus senio, mortis poenam non videre. Insuper ad exemplum, beatum Baptistam Joannem protulerunt, qui in novi Testamenti serie clarissimus effulsit, perque plurima annorum spatia divino mancipatus officio, corpus suum maceravit, donec in Jordanis unda Redemptorem mundi baptizare dignus existeret, atque ipsum Dei Agnum esse digito suo demonstraret.

CAP. V.--Ego vero cum talia eos recitantes audirem, dicebam illis: Quare, seniores mei, vitam et miracula eorum obstupescitis? aut cur illorum facta tam assidue commemoratis? An sunt vobis fortiores, qui desertum habitant, an leviores? At illi respondentes, dixerunt: Fili, fortiores nobis sunt, quia sine adjutorio humano vivunt. Nos itaque alter ab altero conspicimur, pariterque divinum officium a nobis celebratur. Si quando cibum cupimus, paratum reperimus; si quando infirmitas aut aliqua corporis imbecillitas irrepserit, statim cura fratrum cum omni sollicitudine nos adjuvat. In aedificiis lucide constructis habitamus, in quibus et ab aestu solis cooperti sumus, et ab inundatione pluviae, et a turbine venti ac tempestate manemus defensi. Monachi vero, qui in deserto sunt, nihil consolationis nisi a Deo recipiunt. Si quando angustias aut tribulationes perpessi fuerint, vel cum diabolo antiquo humani generis inimico pugnare coeperint, quis eis astat? a quo adjuvantur?

Sed quibus humanum deest solatium, constat eos habere divinum. Et si esuriunt, quis eis panem dabit? Si sitiunt, quis eis aquam tribuit, ubi panis et aqua non est? Maximus labor in desertis locis esse non dubitatur, ubi nihil necessarium reperitur. Primum ergo, quando in solitudine definiunt habitare, in Dei timore certant firmiter stare. In fame et siti, in labore et passione corpora sua cruciant; contra diabolicas insidias viriliter dimicant; et ut vincant, contra tela nequissimi ignea gladiis spiritualibus pugnant. Antiquus etenim ille hostis, totius inventor iniquitatis, studet eos subvertere, et in consortium malitiae suae implicare, atque de bona voluntate, quam inchoabant, retrahere; et mentes eorum mundanis voluptatibus iterum irretire, ut in opere 101 coepto fatiscant persistere. Omnipotens ergo Deus, qui non derelinquit sperantes in se, circumdat eos armis suae potentiae, ut hos incursio Satanae non valeat prosternere, quos protegit celsitudo divinae misericordiae. Quapropter ad eos angeli Dei jugiter mittuntur, ac per manus illorum quaecunque necessaria crebrius eis administrantur. Aquam de petra hauriunt, quod interpretatur Christus. Scriptum est enim: Sancti qui sperant in Domino, habebunt fortitudinem, assument pennas ut aquilae; volabunt, et non deficient; current, et gressus eorum non labentur (Isa. XL). Et alibi: Qui sitiunt, de superno fonte condiuntur, et herbarum folia in ore eorum tanquam favus mellis dulcescunt. Si autem aliquando diabolus adversus eos colluctatur, protinus surgunt: manus suas ad Dominum expandunt, preces ante divinam majestatem fideliter fundunt; mox auxilio coelesti sublevantur, et dolosa jacula inimici penitus destruuntur. Non intelligis, fili, qualiter in Psalmo legitur: Quoniam non in finem oblivio erit pauperis, patientia pauperum non peribit in aeternum (Psal. IX)? Et iterum: Exaudivit eos Dominus in die tribulationis, et de omni angustia liberavit eos (Psal. CVI). Enimvero unusquisque propriam mercedem accipiet, secundum suum laborem (I Cor. III). Beatus est enim vir qui semper est pavidus, et voluntatem Dei in hac praesenti vita et fragili studiosus agit (Prov. XXVIII). Certissime scias, o fili, quoniam angeli Dei sanctis ac justis viris quotidie famulantur, atque virtute superna corpora et animae illorum jugiter illuminantur.

CAP. VI.--Tali denique ratione ego pauper Onuphrius a sanctissimis Patribus in meo monasterio subtiliter instructus, coepi tacita mente tractare quam gloriosa felicitate perfruuntur in coelis qui certamina laboriosa propter amorem Domini tolerarunt in terris: cor meum ardebat, mens mea desiderabiliter fervebat mundi gaudia penitus spernere, patriae coelesti totis viribus appropinquare, sicut Psalmista edocet, dicens: Mihi autem adhaerere Deo bonum est, ponere in Domino Deo spem meam (Psal. LXXII).

CAP. VII.--Dumque haec sollicitus excogitarem, nocte silenti concitus surrexi, parvum panem mecum detuli cum exiguis leguminibus, ut vix usque in quartam diem sufficeret; sicque secundum Dei dispensationem et ejus pietatem profectus sum, ut mihi ostenderet meae habitationis locum. Egrediente autem me de monasterio in montana, veni in desertum; cogitansque ut manerem ibi, continuo lumen splendidum ante me, quasi obvians mihi, vidi. Quo viso, valde timui. Idcirco quoque putavi me debere ad monasterium regredi, unde exivi. Extemplo autem de radio praeclari luminis vir aspectu pulcherrimus accessit ad me, et dixit mihi: Noli pavescere, ego enim sum Dei angelus, tibi ad custodiendum ab ortu tuo providentia divina destinatus, ut jubente Deo tecum manerem, et te in hanc eremum ducerem. Perfectus esto, humilis incede coram Domino, cum gaudio labora, cor tuum in omni custodia conserva, vive sine querela, in bono opere persevera. Ego vero te non derelinquam, donec animam tuam in praesentiam summae majestatis offeram. Haec locutus est mihi angelus, iter inceptum mecum comitatus.

CAP. VIII.--Pergebamus ita simul sex milliaria vel septem, et ad quamdam venimus speluncam nimis decoram. Appropiavi, volens sciscitari, si forte quispiam intus maneret. Secundum consuetudinem monachorum clamare coepi, benedictionem humillime petii. Inde virum sanctissimum exire vidi, quem prostratus humo tenus adoravi. Ille vero manus suas mihi porrexit, de terra me elevavit, osculum mihi pacis tribuit, atque dixit: Tu es enim frater meus, eremiticae cooperator vitae, o fili, ingredere. Deus tibi concedat, ut timor ejus in te permaneat, opus tuum in illius conspectu complaceat. Statim cum eo specum introivi, diesque plures apud illum pausavi, opera ejus cupiens discere, et solitariam habitationem curiosius investigare; ipse quoque ut meum desiderium agnovit, consilium honorabile mihi praebuit; ac qualiter insidias diaboli superare deberem, verbis charitativis gratanter patefecit. Transactis itaque quibusdam diebus, talibus admonuit me verbis, dicens: Fili, surge, mecum perge; interiora deserti debes intrare, et in alia spelunca solus habitare: ibi si viriliter dimicas, omnia daemoniorum tentamenta superas. Idcirco vero Deus in hoc deserto vult te probare, si mandatis ejus fideliter velis obedire.

Fidelia omnia mandata ejus, confirmata in saeculum saeculi, facta in veritate et aequitate (Psal. CX). Vir autem sanctus haec dicens, surrexit, et mecum in interiora deserti iter quatuor dierum perrexit. Quinta vero die devenimus in locum qui Calidiomea dicitur, ibi palmae propinquae erant. Tunc vir Dei inquit: Ecce, fili, vide locum quem tibi Dominus praeparavit ad manendum. Fuit autem ille mecum spatio triginta dierum, edocens me servare cauta diligentia doctrinam Dei mandatorum. Quibus ita peractis, oratione sua sancta Domino 102 me commendavit; et separatus a me, ad propria remeavit. Per singulos vero annos solitus erat me visitare, ac quali industria et simplicitate deberem vivere, divinis alloquiis non cessabat admonere.

CAP. IX.--Quodam autem tempore, juxta consuetudinem ad me veniens, inter verba salutationis prostratus in terram corruit: Dominoque remittens animam, obdormivit. Quod cum viderem, nimis sum contristatus; et devolutus humi, lacrymis obortis uberrime flevi. Corpus ejus mox accepi, et secus Calidiomeam terrae commendavi

CAP. X.--Dum autem ego Paphnutius a viro sanctissimo Onuphrio, rationis hujus loquelam audirem, inquam ad eum: Pater sancte, laborem esse non modicum jam sentio, quem pro nomine Christi tolerasti in hoc eremo. Vir sanctus respondit: Mihi, frater, crede dilectissime: in deserto sustinui, ut saepius putarem me morte superari. Abspes etiam multoties vitae, ut vix halitum in corpore sentirem remanere. Per diem aestu et igne solis ardentis urebar, per noctem rore et pruina infectus, fame et siti defectus. O quanta et qualia passus sum! Non sufficit, neque quempiam decet plagas ac labores enarrare, quos homo moriturus pro Dei viventis amore debet tolerare. Reddet Dominus mercedem laborum sanctorum suorum (Sap. X). Cujus divitiae sicut non augentur, ita nequaquam minuentur. Per quem enim famem, sitim, frigus et aestum, atque multigenarum cruciamenta molestiarum sustinui, potens est cum divitiis coelestibus inter angelorum catervas me consolari: alimenta vero sprevi corporalia, ut dignus acciperem spiritalia. Sanctus enim angelus quotidie panem mihi offerebat, et aquam pro mensura ministrabat, ut corpus meum confortaretur, ne deficeret, et jugiter in laude Dei perseveraret. Arbores palmarum ibidem constitutae erant, quae duodecies in anno dactylorum fructus germinabant. Quos per singulos dies colligens, pro pane edebam, mixtos herbarum foliis, et erant in ore meo tanquam favus mellis. Nam in

Evangelio legitur: Non in solo pane vivit homo, sed in omni verbo quod procedit de ore Dei (Matth. IV). Frater Paphnuti, si implere studes voluntatem Dei, omnia tibi necessaria praeparantur ab eo. Unde ipsa Veritas admonet, dicens: Ne solliciti sitis animae vestrae quid manducetis, aut quid bibatis, neque corpori vestro quid induamini, scit enim Pater vester quia his omnibus indigetis. Quaerite primum regnum Dei, et justitiam ejus, et haec omnia adjicientur vobis (Matth. VI).

CAP. XI.--Cumque hoc a beato viro Onuphrio intentius auscultarem, mirans in sermonibus et actibus ac laboribus illius, dixi: Pater benigne, die Dominico vel Sabbato communionem percipiebas ab aliquo? At ille respondens, ait: Omni die Dominico vel Sabbato angelum Domini paratum invenio, sacrosanctum corpus et sanguinem Domini nostri Jesu Christi secum deferentem: de cujus manu mihi pretiosissima donantur munera, vitaeque meae salus perpetua. Verum etiam omnes qui vitam spiritalem ducunt in eremo monachi tali participantur gaudio. Hi vero sancti eremitae, qui hanc solitudinem habitant, si fortasse aliquando videre hominem desiderant, illico in coelum ab angelo deportantur: visionem illic animae justorum, fulgentium sicut sol in regno Patris eorum, ibi multitudinem contemplantur angelorum, suasque animas coetibus mixtas beatorum. Quare omnes qui in agone contendunt, tota mente, toto corde, totis viribus in bono opere fervent, quatenus gloriam coelestis patriae cum Christo et cum sanctis mereantur possidere. Ista denique omnia, venerando Onuphrio narrante, cognovi juxta summitatem ipsius monticelli, ubi obviavit mihi. Ita videlicet gaudium meum impletum est, ut omnem adversitatem, quam in itinere tuleram, traderem oblivioni.

CAP. XII.--Credo, inquam, Pater, inter felices me deputari, quia videre te et opera tua egregia promerui. Verba tua nimis pulchra, omni dulcedine mellita, ita mei penetrant cordis intima, ut possim dicere cum Psalmista: Quam dulcia faucibus meis eloquia tua, super mel et favum ori meo (Psal. CXVIII)! Qui ait: Fili, mecum vade; locum meae habitationis conspice, parcamus paululum verbis. Continuo surrexit, praeivit, secutus sum. Duxit me secum quasi trium milliariorum iter: venimus Calidiomeam in spiritalem locum, arboribus palmarum gratanter ornatum. Ibi preces Domino fudimus; eisque completis in terram sedimus, in divinis altercantes eloquiis. Sole jamjamque in occasum verso, vidi panem positum cum aqua exigua. Vir etenim Dei sentiens me fatigari, dixit mihi: Profecto, fili, cerno te periclitari, nisi cibum capias. Surge ergo et comede. Cui inquam: Vivit Dominus (III Reg. XVII), et benedictus Dominus Deus meus, in cujus conspectu erimus; non manduco, neque bibo, donec charitate pura pariter cibum sumimus. Igitur vix eum coegi ut faceret quod volui. Verumtamen ut meum agnovit desiderium, panem fregit, tribuit mihi; manducavimus, et saturati sumus 103 nobisque fragmenta superfuerunt edentibus. Noctem illam insomnem pene duximus, divinisque laudibus immorati sumus.

CAP. XIII.--Mane facto, post horam orationis, videbam vultum ejus pallore ita mutatum, et quid acciderit quaesivi ab eo. Qui ait: Non expavescas, frater Paphnuti, quoniam omnipotens Deus recto itinere in hanc solitudinem direxit te, ut honorifice sepelias me, atque corpus meum commendes terrae. Hac etenim hora anima carnis vinculis absolvitur, atque ad creatorem suum in coeleste regnum deportatur. Frater amantissime, (scio namque desiderium tuum) quando redieris in Aegyptum, memorare mei in praesentia fratrum tuorum, et in conspectu omnium Christum colentium. Haec est postulatio mea, quam impetravi a Domino Deo. Si quis oblationem ob amorem nominis mei ante conspectum Domini nostri Jesu Christi, et ad laudem ejus immolat, ab omni tentatione diaboli, et a vinculo pravitatis humanae liber existit, atque cum sanctis angelis in regno coelorum aeternae haereditatis capax fiet. Si quis vero oblationem non valet offerre, vel prae inopia redimere, is in nomine Domini et ad honorem illius eleemosynam pauperi tribuat, et ego orabo pro eo in conspectu Dei, ut dignus in coelestibus vita superna perfrui valeat. Si quis neque oblationem, nec eleemosynam potest offerre, pro charitate mea incensum Domino Deo nostro in odorem suavitatis accendat, et ego rogo pro eo, ut gaudium perenne possideat. Cui inquam: Pater mi, ne irascaris si loquar: Si incensum nec quis habet, nec facultatis aliquid, unde Deum placare potest, ut tamen tua benedictione non careat, in quacunque tribulatione te invocat? Tunc ille respondit: Si quis pauper in deserto, vel in aliquo alio loco oblationem aut eleemosynam, seu incensum non habeat ad immolandum, surgat, et manus suas ad Dominum extendat, ter Dominicam orationem, id est, Pater noster, pro me cum intenta mente, et in nomine sanctae Trinitatis psallat. Ego vero pro ipso ad Dominum intercedo, ut vitae coelestis mereatur particeps fieri cum omnibus sanctis Dei.

CAP. XIV.--Iterum dixi ad eum: Domine, si dignus essem, aut si donis gratiae tuae mihi liceret, post obitum tuum locum istum libentissime obtinerem. At ille ait: Nequaquam tibi, fili, conceditur, nec idcirco misit te Deus in peregrinationem istius solitudinis, ut hic obtineres locum habitationis; sed ut cum justis qui in deserto sunt gratuleris; et intimare ea studeas mundo, quae cognovisti in eremo. In Aegyptum perge: ibi esto usque ad finem vitae tuae; opus bonum perfice, et accipies coronam perpetuae gloriae.

CAP. XV.--Haec cum homo Dei loqueretur, ad volutus sum pedibus ejus, dicens: Pater chare, scio enim quia quidquid petieris a Deo, dabit tibi Dominus propter immensum laborem certaminis longissimi, quo corpus tuum afflixisti septuaginta annis pro nomine Domini; praebe ergo mihi munera tuae sanctae benedictionis, quatenus tibi in virtute efficiar similis, et tua interventione spiritus meus dirigatur, et in futuro tecum participari merear. Qui mox econtra respondens, protulit ista: Paphnuti, ne contristeris: petitio tua, tribuente Domino, erit stabilis. Sta in fide, viriliter age, oculos cum mente ad Deum erige, in mandatis corroborare, bonum facere impiger contende, et vitam aeternam apprehende (I Cor. XVI). Protegant te angeli Dei, et conservent te ab omni consilio pravitatis, ut purus ante Deum et immaculatus in die sui examinis inveniaris. Post haec surrexit, et ad Dominum lacrymans oravit, genua flexit, atque subito dixit: In manus tuas, Deus, commendo spiritum meum. Cumque haec dixisset, lumen splendidum corpus ejus obumbravit, et in ipsius claritate luminis anima sancta carne soluta est.

CAP. XVI.--Repente vero vocem angelorum multorum audivi, laudantium Deum, et in discessu sanctissimae animae sancti Onuphrii, aethera scilicet angelicis canticis resonantia, gaudium ineffabile astris intulerunt, per quem coelestes exercitus animam militis inclyti coelis invexerunt. Mox oculi mei fletu profluunt, interiora gemitus producunt, lacrymarum rivi manarunt, planctus mei miseri Paphnutii exuberant: illud flebilis planxi, quia quem vix inveni, diutius habere non potui. Deinde tunicam meam per dimidium scidi, una parte indutus sum, in alteram collocavi corpus beatum, et sepelivi illud in sepulcro quod excisum erat de petra. Tunc videns me solum remanere, iterum coepi lugere. Ita moerens surrexi, specusque illius habitaculum intrare volui. Denique me astante, ipsa spelunca cecidit cum magna ruina, et palmae radicitus erutae simul procubuerunt. Cognovi itaque ego Paphnutius, quia non esset voluntas

Domini, me in loco illo habitare; secessi inde, in Aegyptum redii: ibique Ecclesiae retuli quae vidi et audivi.

Sanctus igitur Onuphrius obiit mense Junio, die undecimo, id est, III Idus ejusdem mensis. Ibi beneficia ejus praestantur usque in praesentem diem: ad laudem et gloriam Domini nostri Jesu Christi, cui est honor et potestas in saecula saeculorum. Amen.

The Scriptorium Project is the work of a small group of lay people of various apostolic churches who are interested in the preservation, transmission, and translation of the works of the early and medieval church. Our efforts are to make the works of the church fathers accessible to anyone who might have an interest in Christian antiquities and the theological, philosophical, and moral writings that have become the bedrock of Western Civilization.

To-date, our releases have pulled from the Greek, Syriac, Georgian, Latin, Celtic, Ethiopian, and Coptic traditions of Christianity, and have been pulled from sundry local traditions and languages.

Nile River Valley Church Series (Coptic, Nubian, Ethiopian):

Life of Onuphrius by St. Salonius of Geneva (Jan. 2007)
Teaching and Discussion by St. Orsisius of Tabenna (Feb. 2008)
The Holy Ghost by St. Didymas the Blind (Sept. 2008)
Apology Against Theodore by St. Cyril of Alexandria (Nov. 2008)
Rule of St. Macarius by St. Macarius of Egypt (Apr. 2009)
Letter to Leo by St. Proterius of Alexandria (June 2009)
The Paradise of Heraclides by Heraclides of Alexandria (Apr. 2013)
Discourse on Mary Theotokos by St. Cyril of Jerusalem (Sept. 2013)
Nicene Canons in the Old Nubian Language (Jan. 2018)
First Book of Ethiopian Maccabees (Dec 2018)
Life of St. Mary the Egyptian by St. Sophronius of Jerusalem (May 2019)
The Old Nubian Miracle of St. Mena (Jan. 2021)
Two Letters by St. Dionysius of Alexandria (Apr. 2022)
Instructions: Counsel for Novices by St. Ammonas the Hermit (Sept 2022)
Religious Exercise and Quiet by St. Isaiah the Solitary (Oct 2022)
The Vision of Theophilus by St. Cyril of Alexandria (Dec 2022)
Second Book of Ethiopian Maccabees (Aug 2023)
Apophthegmata by St. Macarius of Egypt (Nov. 2023)

www.ingramcontent.com/pod-product-compliance
Lightning Source LLC
LaVergne TN
LVHW061044070526
838201LV00073B/5166